Have You Filled a Bucket Today?

A Guide to Daily Happiness for Kids

By Carol McCloud

Illustrated by David Messing

Bucket Fillosophy

BUCKET FILLOSOPHY® is an imprint of Bucket Fillers, Inc.

PO Box 255, Brighton, MI 48116 • (810) 229-5468

www.bucketfillers101.com

Illustrated by David Messing
Redesigned by Glenn Zimmer
Edited by Kathleen Marusak

Summary: The concept of an invisible bucket and dipper encourages kind and considerate behavior, discourages poor behavior, and teaches the benefits of positive relationships.

Library of Congress Cataloging-in-Publication Data

McCloud, Carol.
Have You Filled a Bucket Today?
A Guide to Daily Happiness for Kids/Carol McCloud
ISBN 978-0-9960999-4-3 Hardcover
ISBN 978-0-9960999-3-6 Softcover
I. McCloud, Carol II. Have You Filled a Bucket Today?
A Guide to Daily Happiness for Kids
1. Child Development
2. Behavior
3. Kindness
4. Happiness
5. Social Skills
Library of Congress Control Number: 2015912365

10 9 8 7 6 5 4 3

Author's Dedication

This revised and updated book is dedicated to all bucket fillers, past, present, and future, who add beauty and joy to life by simply filling buckets.

Author's Acknowledgments

In the 1960s, Dr. Donald O. Clifton (1924-2003) first created the "Dipper and Bucket" story that has now been passed along for decades. Dr. Clifton later went on to co-author the #1 *New York Times* bestseller *How Full is Your Bucket?* and was named the Father of Strengths Psychology.

A portion of the proceeds from this book is being donated to The Salvation Army, an organization that for more than one hundred years has served and modeled love and compassion for others.

Introduction by Author Carol McCloud

This book was first published in 2006 to teach young children, primarily ages 4-9, how to be bucket fillers. Since then, bucket filling has spread around the world to help millions of people of all ages have happier and more rewarding lives. In this revised and updated edition, the verbs "bucket dipping" and "bullying" have replaced the nouns "bucket dipper" and "bully" to help readers understand that "bucket dipping" and "bullying" are negative behaviors (what we are doing) and not permanent labels (who we are). Readers will also learn that you can fill or dip into your own bucket.

I first learned about bucket filling in a seminar for early childhood educators in the 1990s. The speaker, a brain research expert, said it is helpful to think of every person as being born with an invisible bucket. The bucket represents a person's mental and emotional health. You can't see the bucket, but it's there. She said that it is primarily the responsibility of parents and other caregivers to fill a child's bucket. When you hold, caress, nurture, touch, sing, play, and provide loving attention, safety, and care, you fill a child's bucket. Giving that love is filling buckets.

In addition to being loved, children must also be taught how to love others. Children who learn how to express kindness and love lead happier lives. When you care about others and show that love by what you say and do, you feel good and you fill your own bucket, too.

As you read this book with children, use it as an opportunity to model this concept by filling their buckets. Tell them why they are special to you. Help them imagine whose bucket they might fill and what they could say or do to fill a bucket. Tell them whose bucket you filled that day. Practice with them to become daily bucket fillers. Very quickly they will experience the pride and joy of filling buckets.

Learn more about bucket filling through our website, **www.bucketfillers101.com**, and be sure to sign up for our free e-newsletter, BUCKET FILLOSOPHY® 101. Keep filling buckets and your bucket will always be full.

All day long, everyone in the whole wide world walks around carrying an invisible bucket.

You can't see it, but it's there.

5

You have a bucket.
Each member of your family has a bucket.

Your grandparents, friends, and neighbors all have buckets.

Everyone carries an invisible bucket.

Your bucket has one purpose only.

Its purpose is to hold your good thoughts and good feelings about yourself.

You feel happy and good
when your bucket is full,

and you feel sad and lonely
when your bucket is empty.

Other people feel the
same way, too.

They're happy when their buckets are full
and they're sad when their buckets are empty.

It's great to have a full bucket and this is how it works . . .

Other people can fill your bucket and you can fill theirs.
You can fill your own bucket, too.
So, how do you fill a bucket?

You fill a bucket when you show love to someone, when you say or do something kind, or even when you give someone a smile.

That's being a bucket filler.

A bucket filler is a loving, caring person who says and does nice things to make others feel special.

When you treat others with kindness and respect, you fill their bucket.

But, you can also dip into a bucket and take out some good feelings.
You dip into a bucket when you make fun of someone, when you
say or do mean things, or even when you ignore someone.

That's bucket dipping.

Bullying is bucket dipping.

**When you hurt others, you dip into their bucket.
You will dip into your own bucket, too.**

Many people who dip have an empty bucket.
They may think they can fill their own bucket
by dipping into someone else's . . .
but that will never work.

You never fill your own bucket when you dip into someone else's.

But guess what?
When you fill someone's bucket,
you fill your own bucket, too!

You feel good when you help others feel good.

All day long, we are either filling up or
dipping into each other's buckets by
what we say and what we do.

Try to fill a bucket and see what happens.

You love your mom and dad. Why not tell them you love them?
You can even tell them why.

Your caring words will fill their buckets with joy.

Watch for smiles to light up their faces. You will feel like smiling, too. A smile is a good clue that you have filled a bucket.

If you practice, you'll become a great bucket filler.

Just remember that everyone carries an invisible bucket,
and think of what you can say or do to fill it.

Here are some ideas for you.
You could smile and say "Hi!" to the bus driver.

He has a bucket, too.

You could invite the new kid at school to play with you.

23

You could write a thank-you note to your teacher.

You could tell your grandpa that you like spending time with him.

There are many ways to fill a bucket.

Bucket filling is fun and easy to do.
It doesn't matter how young or old you are.
It doesn't cost money.
It doesn't take much time.

And remember, when you fill someone else's bucket,
you fill your own bucket, too.

When you're a bucket filler, you make your home, your school, and your neighborhood better places for all.

Bucket filling makes everyone feel good.

So, why not decide to be a bucket filler today and every day?
Just start each day by saying to yourself,

"I'm going to do something to fill someone's bucket today."

And, at the end of each day, ask yourself,
"Did I fill a bucket today?"

"Yes, I did!" That's the life of a bucket filler . . .

And that's YOU!

About the Author

Carol McCloud, the Bucket Lady, and her Bucket Fillers Team teach the importance of bucket filling to educators, businesses, community groups, churches, and children. As an early childhood specialist, Carol understands that patterns affecting self-worth start very early in life and are fostered by others. Carol is president of Bucket Fillers, Inc., an educational organization in Brighton, Michigan, whose mission is to create bucketfilling families, schools, workplaces, and communities. She lives in Venice, Florida with her husband, Jack.
Visit www.bucketfillers101.com.

About the Illustrator

David Messing is a life-long artist, illustrator, cartoonist, sculptor, writer, and instructor. For thirty years, Dave, along with his wife, Sandy, and in more recent years their boys, Scott, Kevin, and Adam, have taught in their family-owned art school. Although Dave spent many years designing and building props, sets, and miniatures for film and print commercials and almost every auto manufacturer, his current passion is cartooning and book illustration.
Visit www.coroflot.com/davemessing.